STUDENT COURSEPACK SERIES

PREHISTORY

ELIZABETH MILLER

Student and Teacher Edition

Prehistory Coursepack
Student and Teacher Edition

Elizabeth Miller

Dear Teacher,

Thank you for your purchase of this coursepack. This version contains the Teacher Coursepack with all answers and notes filled in, followed by the reproducible Student Coursepack. As a teacher myself, I know that your time and money are valuable. Therefore, I hope that this coursepack will save you time in developing a whole course from scratch.

This coursepack can be used in a variety of ways depending on the structure of your class.

I originally developed it for use in my flipped classroom. I had created most of the notes and lectures, but wanted an easier way for students to pace themselves and be sure they were pulling the needed information from the lectures. Towards the start of the coursepack you will see a checklist with "Due Dates." I use this to allow student some autonomy. At the start of each week they are assigned 2-3 lectures to watch at home as well as the corresponding quizzes. As they complete the lectures and the work to go with them they initial it on their checklist. This allows them to work ahead as they wish, but keeps everyone at a minimum pace. Students do all work outside of school in their coursepack and bring it in on Fridays. I found having everything in one place was invaluable for students who struggle with organization. If I'm being honest it is also very helpful for me. Although photocopying that much at once is time consuming, once I do that, I'm done for the unit! In this case- four weeks! More information on using this as part of a flipped classroom can be found in my book, *Flipping History: How to Start Flipping Your Classroom Today*.

However, this coursepack is not just for those teachers flipping their classroom. You can also use it in a traditional classroom as guided notes during direct instruction. The scaffolded notes allow students to fill in notes as your lecture progresses. The fill-ins will keep your students on track, while allowing them to focus on what you are saying, rather than writing everything down. For classes with students working at various speeds and levels you can give those students who struggle to keep pace the teacher version (filled-in) and have them highlight key concepts. As the year progresses you can move them towards the scaffolded notes. Most students will use the scaffolded notes. Superior note takers can use regular notebook paper to take full notes, but check them against your teacher copy as needed. In this way you can address multiple needs during one lecture. The additional work (questions, flashcards, etc) can be assigned for homework or as independent and group work during class.

Feel free to pick and choose which parts of the coursepack work for you in your classroom. For example, while I like to assign a Critical Reading to my students each week, you may not. Additionally, my checklist format may not make sense for you and your students. If you just want to use the scaffolded notes- that's fine too!

While I like to give all of the notes and assignments at once to students, you may want to give out the notes with each lecture. My hope is that this will be a useful supplement to what you are already doing, not a hard rule as to what should be done!

Best of Luck,

Elizabeth

A few notes:

- Due to copyright restrictions I could not include the original articles I used for the "Critical Reading" assignments. The citation may be found in the Teacher's Version (along with the answers based on that specific article). All of the articles I use are available for free and could be found with a quick Google search of the citation. That being said, feel free to use whatever articles you find relevant and interesting for your students! My goal was to help them connect what we were learning about in history, with current events in today's world.

- Presentations to accompany all of the notes in this coursepack are available at pennyuniversitypress.com. You can always make your own as well!

- If you are interested in purchasing just the Prehistory Student Coursepack in bulk for your class, please contact me at elizabeth@pennyuniversitypress.com
- Feel free to reproduce the material in this book as needed for your classroom, but please refrain from using it for anything other than educational purposes.
- If you find the materials enclosed useful, please consider leaving a review on Amazon.com so that other educators can find this resource as well!

Please feel free to contact me with any questions, I always love connecting and sharing with other educators!

Coursepack

Teacher's Edition
PREHISTORY
Introduction

Archaeology

&

Early Man

Coursepack Components

- **Two Column Notes**: These make up the bulk of our coursepack. They are guided notes that correspond with each video lecture that you listen to. You should listen to a lecture once, pausing the screen to fill in your notes, and then listen to the lecture again all the way through for understanding.

- **Review Questions**: These may be found at the end of a lecture, group of lectures, or unit. You need to answer all review questions to the best of your ability. The answers should be located within your notes and lecture videos. You should answer them directly in your coursepack.

- **Flashcards**: You will periodically see "Flaschards" at the end of a lecture or with review questions. You should create a flashcard for each term listed and place it on your flashcard ring. The instructions for how to create flashcards specifically for history class can be found on the next page. You should create flashcards as you come across them in the courespack.

- **Maps, drawings, textboxes, etc:** Throughout the coures you will see activities where you may be asked to answer a question, fill in a map, or draw something, these are not optional and should be completed with the lecture that they are within.

- **Critical Reading**: Every other week you have a Critical Reading or CR that you need to complete. You will be assigned an article from a variety of places (NYT, Smithsonian) that you are to read and fill out the CR Assignment page in your courespack for. On Fridays we will have a class discussion about your CR so it is very important that you complete them on time. Instructions for completing a CR can be found in the following pages.

- **Internet Literacy**: On weeks where you do not have a CR you will have an Internet Literacy Worksheet or an IL. These worksheets are designed to improve your internet skills such as using a search engine or finding reputable sources. We will go over them on Fridays so they need to be completed on time.

- **Due Dates/Signatures**: These checklists found at the front of each coursepack are designed to keep you on track and make sure you get things done by the due date. Check assignments off as you complete them and then have your parent/guardian sign off when they are done.

- If you keep up to date with your coursepack work you will find your history work very straightforward and easily completed. Please come to me with any questions or concerns.

- If you misplace this courespack, you are responsible to print out a new one, and fill it in. Courespacks must be turned in, fully filled in, at the end of a unit, so it is very important you do not lose it. You should treat it like a text book, and bring it with you to class each day.

How to complete a Critical Reading

- **Citation:** *A citation for the article you read using Chicago MLA format.* We will be going over this in class, but this is a sample: (I'll include a sample for them)

- **Summary**: *2 (and only 2) sentences summarizing the major point that the author is making in the reading.* Believe it or not you will find it difficult to summarize something in only 2 sentences, you need to make sure you really understand the main point that the author is trying to make.

- **Critical Insight:** *2-3 sentences describing something that you learned from the reading or a new insight that you gained.* It could be something that you already knew, but now you understand better, if that is the case tell me why you understand it better now. What information did the author present that sparked your interest or made you think?

- **Critical Question**: *A question you have after completing the reading.* It could be a critique of what the author has said (something you agreed with or did not agree with), or something further that you would like to know. This should be a well thought out question, not one that can be answered by the reading. It should be an open ended question (not a yes or no question). This is the most important part of the CR assignment as it forms the basis for our class discussions.

How to make Flashcards for History

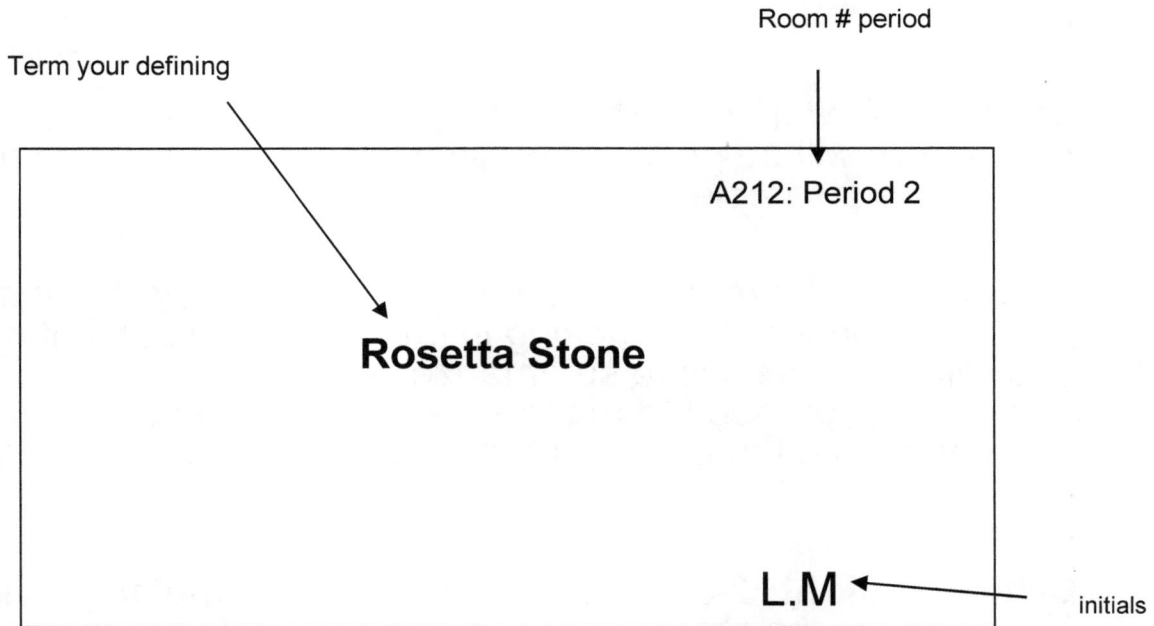

Room # period

Term your defining

A212: Period 2

Rosetta Stone

L.M ← initials

Unit of study: lecture the term came from

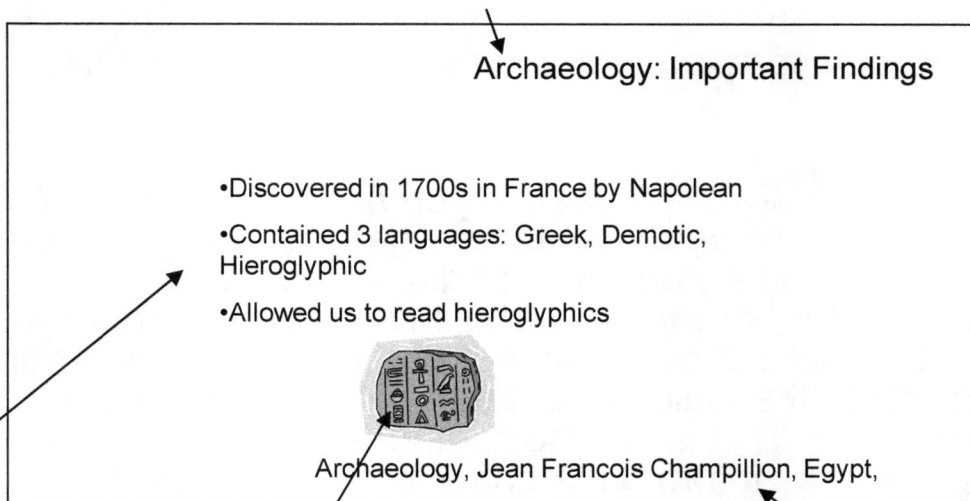

Archaeology: Important Findings

•Discovered in 1700s in France by Napolean

•Contained 3 languages: Greek, Demotic, Hieroglyphic

•Allowed us to read hieroglyphics

Archaeology, Jean Francois Champillion, Egypt,

Comprehensive definition.
Not just what it is, but why its
important

Other flashcards
associated with
this one

Picture you associated with
term; can be stick figures; for
example you might draw a
crown if the flashcard was a
king

Checklists: Weeks 1 and 2 Intro and Archaeology

Due _____

The Social Sciences
____ Lecture
____ Notes
____ Quiz

Skills of an Historian
____ Lecture
____ Notes
____ Quiz

Tools of an Historian
____ Lecture
____ Notes
____ Quiz

____ CR Reading   ____
Flashcards
____ Section Reviews ____ DT
I commented ____ times.

Due _____

Archaeology Overview
____ Lecture
____ Notes
____ Quiz

Important Findings
____ Lecture
____ Notes
____ Quiz

No third lecture this week.

____ IL Worksheet   ____
Flashcards
____ Section Reviews ____ DT
I commented ____ times.

Parent Signature:
_____

Mastery Test 1 Mastered on _____

Teacher Signature: _____

Checklist: Weeks 3 and 4 Early Man

Due _____

Very Early Man
- ___ Lecture
- ___ Notes
- ___ Quiz

Old Stone Age
- ___ Lecture
- ___ Notes
- ___ Quiz

Neanderthals
- ___ Lecture
- ___ Notes
- ___ Quiz

___ CR Reading   ___ Flashcards
___ Section Reviews ___ DT
I commented ____ times.

Due _____

Cro-Magnon Man
- ___ Lecture
- ___ Notes
- ___ Quiz

Cave Paintings
- ___ Lecture
- ___ Notes
- ___ Quiz

Neolithic Revolution
- ___ Lecture
- ___ Notes
- ___ Quiz

___ CR Reading   ___ Flashcards
___ Section Reviews ___ DT
I commented ____ times.

Parent Signature:
_____

Mastery Test 2 Mastered on _____

Teacher Signature: _____

Question of the Day

Monday:

Tuesday:

Wednesday:

Thursday:

Friday:

Critical Reading

Citation:

Pogrebin, R. (2006, April 1). $200 million gift prompts a debate over antiquities. *The New York Times*. Retrieved from http://www.nytimes.com/2006/04/01/arts/

Summary:

Shelby White donated $200 million dolalrs to NYU to start an ancient studies institute. Many archaeologists are afraid that this money will be used to buy artifacts that were originally stolen from the countries they were found in, some professors are resigning in protest.

Critical Insight:

I had no idea that so many famous things in museums were originally stolen from other countries. It seems like a big issue if people are resigning and willing to turn down $200 million over it. The White's seem to mean well but this appears to be a big debate between archaeologists and art collectors.

Critical Question:

What happens if they are able to prove that an artifact was stolen from a country a long time ago but an art collector that had nothing to do with the theft thought they were purchasing it legitimately, should it go back?

The Social Sciences

History

- What happened?
    - the story of the world's people once writing was developed
    - before written history = prehistory

Geography

- Where it happened
    - how earth's features influenced settlements and the course of history

Economics

- Systems of Money $$
    - how people make their living
    - agricultural vs. industrial countries
        - Agricultural = farm based
        - Industrial = industry based
    - have vs. have-nots
    - G.N.P
        - GNP = Gross National Product

Sociology

- Society and culture
    - how people's behavior affects the world

Political Science

- Government and civics
    - how people rule themselves
    - how to be a good citizen

Anthropology

- Study of the origins and development of man through the study of fossils, artifacts, tools, etc.
- tries to explain where man came from

Skills of an Historian

Interpret fact vs. opinion	- Fact = statement that can be proven o Opinion = your view of a situation (cannot be proven)
Draw conclusions	- Using what you learn plus what you already know to guess what happened or what will happen next
See Cause and Effect	- Historical events do not happen independently o Actions always have repercussions
Recognize Points of View	- Two people may see the same event happen differently o Gender, social status, economics, geographical location and other things effect POV

Identify bias and prejudice	- Historical thinking can be clouded by our modern day judgments
	  o Bias = being partial, using pre-judgment to form opinion
	  o Prejudice = any preconceived opinion or feeling, either favorable or unfavorable.

Tools of an Historian

Primary Sources

- Are materials created in the past by people living at the time,
  - including photographs, paintings, documents, advertisements, music, films, and objects

Secondary Sources

- Are writings by historians and others who use available sources to interpret the past.
  - They provide analysis and summary, placing events, people and evidence in historical context and asking questions about their meaning and significance

Time Lines

- Show how events occur chronologically
- B.C/B.C.E → "0"
  - Years work towards "0"
  - B.C. = Before Christ
  - B.C.E = Before Common Era
- A.D./C.E "0" →
  - Years work away from "0"
  - A.D. = Anno Domini
  - C.E. = Common Era

Maps

Graphs

Charts

Section Review

Flashcards: History, Geography, Economics, Sociology, Political Science, Anthropology, Fact, Opinion, Bias, Point of View, Primary Source, Secondary Source

1.   Why is it important to study fields such as Political Science and Economics? How do these fields help us to understand history better?

All of these things impact what happens to people and their societies. If we want to understand why an historical event occurred, we need to understand what was going on in government, with people's jobs, and in their culture at the time.

2.   Why is it important for an historian to be able to identify biases and prejudices? How do these things alter historical interpretations?

It is important to understand bias and predjudice when reading eye witness accounts as well as diaries, etc. These things are told from one person's view point and may not be an accurate representation of how everyone felt. They may be very one sided. Historians themselves have bias and predjudice, and this may also effect how they decide to present information, so we always need to be on the look out for these things and cross check everything.

3.   What is a primary source? How does it differ from a secondary source?

A primary source is something created in the past by people living at the time. A secondary source is when a historian gathers information from several sources and puts it all together and analyzes it. An example of a primary source would be a photograph, an example of a secondary source would be a textbook.

4.   Explain how two people can witness the same event, but give a completely different interpretation of what happened? How does this come into play when we read an historians analysis of an event?

Two people can see the same event bery differently based on what their life's experience has been. For example if a wealthy roman and a roman slave both left diaries, their reaction to a new law about slavery would be very different because they see it differently. Historians have to remember this because the way one person described something might not be how everybody saw it.

Questions of the Day

Monday:

Tuesday:

Wednesday:

Thursday:

Friday:

Archaeology

Archaeology

- The study of the remains of past human life and cultures
  - Began ~ 500 years ago
  - Europeans dug up Greek/Roman artifacts and sold them

Artifacts

- Things made by people
  - Help us learn how people lived long ago
  - Helps when no written records can be found
- Do NOT have to be works of art
  - Every day items
    - Tools, weapons, pottery
  - Earliest artifacts = chipped rocks

Site

- Location where a "dig" is to take place
  - Archaeologists work closely with governments to make sure it is OK to dig
  - Permits must be given

Excavate

- To dig into the earth; uncover remains of past

Date

- To find the age of remains
  - J. Thomsen first to divide human history into ages

Archaeology cont.

Ages

- Used to divide early human history
- Based on the material people used for tools and weapons
  - Stone Age
    - Divided into old, middle, new
  - Bronze Age
  - Iron Age

Change in Division

- Archaeologists decided how people got food = more important than materials for tools
  - Early history divided into two periods
    - Food gatherers
    - Food producers

Tree Rings

- First way scientists dated archaeological finds
  - Each year a tree grows a new ring

Stop and Check for Understanding:

Flashcards: Archaeology, fossil, artifacts, site, excavate, dating, ages

How do archaeologists divide early human history?

They divide it by the material they made tools out of, and how they got their food.

Important Findings

Italy in 1700s

- Discovery of two cities buried by the eruption of Mt. Vesuvius in A.D. 79.
  - Herculaneum
  - Pompeii
    - Evidence found of how early Romans actually lived.

Rosetta Stone

- Discovered in Rosetta, Egypt by Napoleon's troops
  - Inscribed w/ 3 languages
    - Greek
    - Demotic (everyday Egyptian)
    - Hieroglyphics (religious Egyptian)
- Deciphered by Jean-Francois Champollion
  - it was the record of a law written in 196 B.C. praising King Ptolomy V.

Olduvai Gorge

- Site in Tanzania
  - Human fossils more than 2 million years old
  - Footprints found to be 3.7 million years old
  - Remains of 12 year old boy

What three languages were on the Rosetta Stone?

The three languages were Greek, Demotic, and Hieroglyphics.

Olduvai Gorge

Color in the Map above and use an atlas or the internet to label as may of the following as you can (you should at least label Olduvai Gorge).

1) Taung, 2) West Turkana, 3) East Turkana, 4) Olduvai Gorge, 5) Peninj, 6) Hadar, 7) Laetoli, 8) Sterkfontein, 9) Swartkrans

Section Review

Flashcards: Pompeii, Vesuvius, Rosetta Stone, Olduvai Gorge

What is the difference between a fossil and an artifact?
A fossil is the remains of something that was living, an artifact is something that was man made.

What is the difference between an archaeologist and an anthropologist?
An archaeologist studies the remains of past human life, such as bones. They try to determine when a fossil was in existence. An anthropologist studies artifacts and tries to figure out how and why man went where he did.

What two cities, later discovered in the 1700s, were buried by Mt. Vesuvius?
1. Pompeii
2. Herculaneum

Name one example of "dating" that scientists and archeologists use to find out how old an artifact is:
Some scientists use "three rings" each year a tree grows a new ring, so they can count backwards to figure out how old something is.

What is the Rosetta Stone? What two major languages were on it? Why was it important?
It was a stone discovered in the 1700s that had Greek and Egyptian on it. It allowed us to translate hieroglyphics for the first time.

Question of the Day

Monday:

Tuesday:

Wednesday:

Thursday:

Friday:

Critical Reading

Citation:

Wilford, J. N. (2012, April 8). New fossils indicate early branching of human family tree. *The New York Times.* Retrieved from newyorktimes.com

Summary:

The discovery of three new fossils might mean that there were at least two other types of homo species living at the same time as homo erectus. Different scientists have different opinions on the fossils.

Critical Insight:

Scientists think there were more than one species of humans that lived in ancient Africa. The human tree has a lot more branches than the history books make it seem. It seems like the skull and jaw of fossils are really important to figuring out what type of species they are.

Critical Question:

Can scientists ever know for certain how many species there were? With each discovery will that change what they are currently thinking?

Very Early Man

65 Million Years Ago

- Humans did NOT live during the same time as dinosaurs
- Dinosaurs died out

3 Million Years Ago

- The first human like hominids appear
- The planet was teaming with life, 3 examples are:
    - Answers vary
    - Answers vary
    - Answers vary

Very Early Humans

- Higher primates including apes and early man first appear
- There were important differences between the two:
    - Early humans could stand upright
        - Apes could not
    - Their hands were different
        - Apes hands were made for climbing and swinging
        - Human hands were jointed so that they could use tools

Lucy

- Discovered in 1974 on the continent of Africa
- 3 million years ago she would have been 4 feet tall and weighed 50 llb
- She probably died from drowning in a lake

Fossils and Artifacts

- Fossils are remains of living things (plants, animals, people), **not** man made
- Artifacts are remains of things that were man made **not** living things

Old Stone Age

Handy Man
(Homo Habilis)

- One of the first hominids to use tools
- These people got their food from hunting and gathering
  - They did not plant crops, instead they gathered:
    - nuts
    - fruits

- taller and smarter than Lucy's people
- Did not know how to make fire

Upright Man
(Homo Erectus)

- did know how to make fire, important because:
  - Now people could cooktheir food
  - People gathered around the fire each night and shared stories of the days hunt
    - = development of community

- Same size as modern humans
- Better tools including:
  - Axe and knife
- Did not have to worry about freezing
- Made clothes from animal skins_

Man Leaves Home

- About 1 million years ago, man leaves Africa
- The Ice Age allowed them to walk over giant frozen walkways

---

Flashcards: Lucy, Handy Man (Homo Habilis), Upright Man (Homo Erectus), Ice Age

Why was the ability to make fire so important?

Neanderthals

Neanderthals (Homo Sapien)

- Homo sapiens
  - Means "man who thinks"
- Appeared about 300,000 years ago
- Named for the river in Germany where remains were first discovered
  - Have also been found throughout parts Asia and Africa
  - ~1 million thought to be living at the time

Good Hunters

- Used traps to catch birds and small animals
- Used pitfalls to catch large animals
  - Pitfall = large hole covered with branches
  - Once animal fell in they would kill it with a spear

Better Builders

- Made houses by covering framework of mammoth bones with animal skins
  - Bones piled on the bottom prevented them from blowing away
  - As many as 30 people lived in a house during cold months
- Improved cave dwellings by digging drainage ditches and covering entrances w/ rocks

Religion

- First people to bury their dead

Flashcards: Neanderthal (Homo Sapien), Pitfall, Bury the Dead

How did Neanderthals improve their living conditions?

They used traps to catch food, they built better houses that were more comfortable and protected, and they used better materials to construct things.

Question of the Day

Monday:

Tuesday:

Wednesday:

Thursday:

Friday:

Cro-Magnon Man

Cro-Magnon Man (EEMH)
- Named after a rock shelter in France where remains were discovered in 1868
- Appeared in North Africa, Asia, and Europe
- Appeared ~100,000 years ago
- Considered the first modern human beings

Skilled Tool Makers
- Invented the burin
  - Ancient chisel
    - Used to make other tools
- Used bone, ivory, shells and wood for tools

Better Hunters
- Used antler bones to create sharper spears
  o Could fly faster and farther
  o Could stay greater distance from animals = safer
- **Better Hunters → increased food supply→ bigger population**

Invention of the Axe
- Used to cut down trees and hollow out logs for canoes
- In SE Asia used to cut bamboo for rafts
- Boats allowed them to travel on ocean
  - Most likely how they reached Australia ~ 40,000 years ago

Art
- Carved statues out of ivory and clay
- Created jewelry out of shells
  - Decorated clothing with ivory beads
- Made _____ and played music from hollowed out bones

Working as a Group
- Hunted in large _____
- Gathered yearly to exchange information about the movement of animals and to trade _____

See next lecture for Cave Paintings

Cave Paintings

Cave Paintings	• Many caves throughout Europe, Africa, and South America have been found – Covered w/ brightly colored paints made from minerals • Pictures show mostly animals such as horses, bulls, and deer • Many anthropologists think they have religions significance
Religion	• Believed that animals had spirits • Painting a picture gave people power over the spirit – This would help them find and kill the animal • Some cave paintings depict ceremonies, traditions, and history
Lascaux, France	• Discovered by accident in 1940 • Children playing in a field stumbled across the opening to a cave, inside the walls were covered with drawings •

Explore the Lascaux cave website. Choose 1 "panel" from the cave (for example the Hall of the Bulls). Write a story below about what you think is happening in the picture. Use lots of details and creativity. You may draw the picture to go with it if you wish.

Answers will vary

Section Review

Flashcards: Cro-Magnon Man, Burin, Lascaux France, Cave painting, Invention of Axe

1. What is a hunter-gatherer?

Hunter-gatherers do not stay in one place and grow food. Instead they hunt for animals and gather wild berries and nuts. This means they must move where the food is.

2. What is a Stone Age?

The stone age defines the time period in which prehistoric man made tools using stone. Some stone age people include Homo erectus and homo habilis.

3. Why was the ability to make fire so important?

Making fire meant that man could cook his food to reduce disease. He could also stay in one place longer. He no longer worried about freezing to death. Finally it helped to build a sense of community since people would tell stories around it.

4. How could early humans travel from Africa to Australia without a boat?

It was the ice age so people were able to walk over great ice bridges that would later become rivers and oceans.

5. What did Cro-Magnon man paint on cave walls?

He mainly painted animals and things in nature. He rarely painted people.

6. Why did Cro-Magnon man paint on cave walls?

We're not really sure, it might have been to let other groups of people know where they found food. It also may have been religious. He may have drawn the animal he killed to represent the animal's spirit. It may have been a right of passage, it's a mystery still.

Neolithic Age

Neolithic Revolution	• c. 8000 B.C.E People changed from food gatherers to food producers
	• 2 Important discoveries:
	  ○ Grow Food
	  ○ Herd Animals

Agriculture	• Developed independently in different parts of the world • People discovered that seed from wild grains could be planted and harvested
Herders	• First happened when hunting bands built fences to enclose wild animals • Farmers could kill one animal at a time and save the rest for later • Captured animals began to lose their fear of people, this led to domestication
Food Producers	• Once people became producers they built permanent settlements
Early Villages	• Had 150-200 people in areas with good soil and water supplies

Neolithic Age cont.

Earliest Villages

- Jericho (present day Israel)
  - Dates to 8000 BCE
- Abu Hureyra (present day Syria)
  - Dates to 7500 BCE
- Catal Huyuk (present day Turkey)
  - Dates from 6500-5700 BCE

Catal Huyuk

- Struck by fire which blackened wooden and cloth objects
  - Helped preserve the objects

Early Houses

- Houses were made of sun-dried mud brick with flat roofs
- They used *post-and-lintels* to support the roof
- Each house had 2 or 3 rooms and no door
  - People went in and out through a hole in the roof

Specialization

- The development of occupations
- Fewer people were needed to produce food so other jobs developed
  - Cloth weaving
  - Metal work

Neolithic Age cont.

Village Government

- Land ownership develops and with it the protection of property

Chief

- Disputes were settled by a single chief who also along with a small group directed village activities
- Chiefs also served as village priests

Prayer

- At first Neolithic people prayed to forces of nature
- Later they developed gods and goddesses
  - Earth Mother was the most important, many houses had alters to her

Look up the word "revolution" in the dictionary or at dictionary.com. What does this word mean? Write a brief paragraph discussing whether or not the Neolithic Revolution was indeed a revolution. What other term could be used to describe this era?

Answers will vary

Early Man Review

Flashcards: Neolithic Age, Neolithic Revolution, Paleolithic Age, Prehistory, Specialization, domesticated Civilization, Post-and-lintel, Earth Mother

1. What two important discoveries changed people from food gatherers to food producers?

    The ability to grow food and the ability to herd animals.

2. What were two results of the increased food supply during the Neolithic age?

    Increased food supplies mean that the population increased that people no longer had to work so hard to get food, so they could have specialization of jobs.

3. What two roles did village chiefs play?

    They were rulers and priests.

4. How did learning to produce food lead to developing villages by early civilizations?

    Once people could produce food, farming and herding, provided a steady food supply and people no longer needed to hunt and gather food. This meant that they could stay in one place instead of following the herds.

Prehistory Coursepack
Student Edition

_____'s
Coursepack

PREHISTORY
Introduction
Archaeology
&
Early Man

Coursepack Components

- **Two Column Notes**: These make up the bulk of our coursepack. They are guided notes that correspond with each video lecture that you listen to. You should listen to a lecture once, pausing the screen to fill in your notes, and then listen to the lecture again all the way through for understanding.

- **Review Questions**: These may be found at the end of a lecture, group of lectures, or unit. You need to answer all review questions to the best of your ability. The answers should be located within your notes and lecture videos. You should answer them directly in your coursepack.

- **Flashcards**: You will periodically see "Flaschards" at the end of a lecture or with review questions. You should create a flashcard for each term listed and place it on your flashcard ring. The instructions for how to create flashcards specifically for history class can be found on the next page. You should create flashcards as you come across them in the coursepack.

- **Maps, drawings, textboxes, etc**: Throughout the coures you will see activities where you may be asked to answer a question, fill in a map, or draw something, these are not optional and should be completed with the lecture that they are within.

- **Critical Reading**: Every other week you have a Critical Reading or CR that you need to complete. You will be assigned an article from a variety of places (NYT, Smithsonian) that you are to read and fill out the CR Assignment page in your courespack for. On Fridays we will have a class discussion about your CR so it is very important that you complete them on time. Instructions for completing a CR can be found in the following pages.

- **Internet Literacy**: On weeks where you do not have a CR you will have an Internet Literacy Worksheet or an IL. These worksheets are designed to improve your internet skills such as using a search engine or finding reputable sources. We will go over them on Fridays so they need to be completed on time.

- **Due Dates/Signatures**: These checklists found at the front of each coursepack are designed to keep you on track and make sure you get things done by the due date. Check assignments off as you complete them and then have your parent/guardian sign off when they are done.

- If you keep up to date with your coursepack work you will find your history work very straightforward and easily completed. Please come to me with any questions or concerns.

- If you misplace this courespack, you are responsible to print out a new one, and fill it in. Courespacks must be turned in, fully filled in, at the end of a unit, so it is very important you do not lose it. You should treat it like a text book, and bring it with you to class each day.

How to complete a Critical Reading

- **Citation:** *A citation for the article you read using Chicago MLA format.* We will be going over this in class, but this is a sample: (I'll include a sample for them)

- **Summary**: *2 (and only 2) sentences summarizing the major point that the author is making in the reading.* Believe it or not you will find it difficult to summarize something in only 2 sentences, you need to make sure you really understand the main point that the author is trying to make.

- **Critical Insight:** *2-3 sentences describing something that you learned from the reading or a new insight that you gained.* It could be something that you already knew, but now you understand better, if that is the case tell me why you understand it better now. What information did the author present that sparked your interest or made you think?

- **Critical Question**: *A question you have after completing the reading.* It could be a critique of what the author has said (something you agreed with or did not agree with), or something further that you would like to know. This should be a well thought out question, not one that can be answered by the reading. It should be an open ended question (not a yes or no question). This is the most important part of the CR assignment as it forms the basis for our class discussions.

How to make Flashcards for History

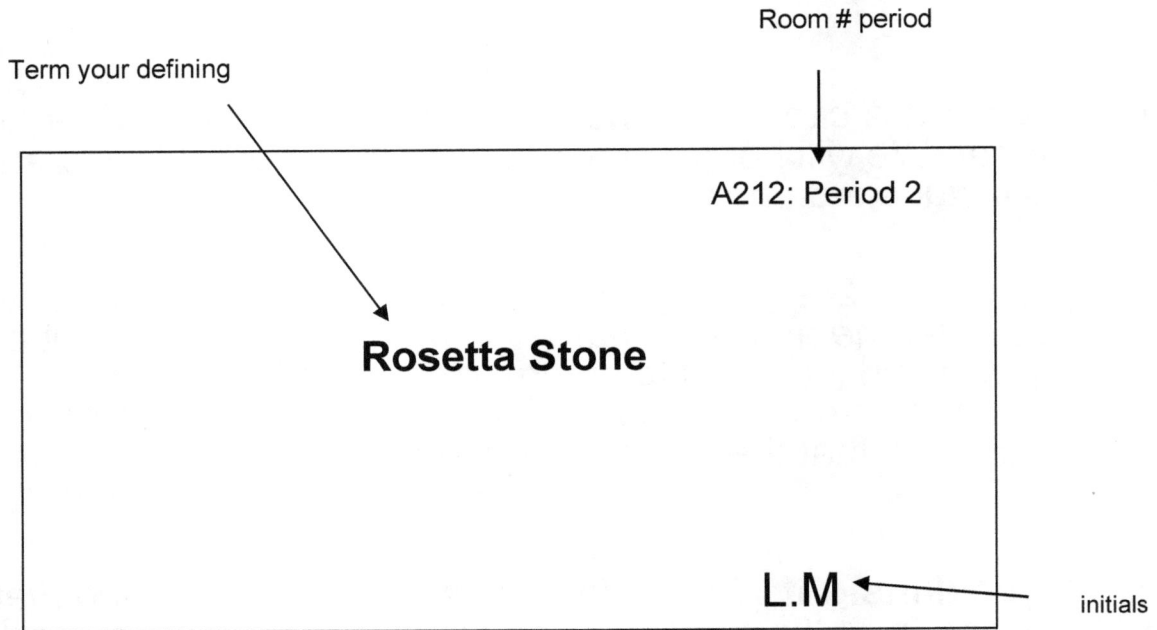

Room # period

Term your defining

A212: Period 2

Rosetta Stone

L.M ← initials

Unit of study: lecture the term came from

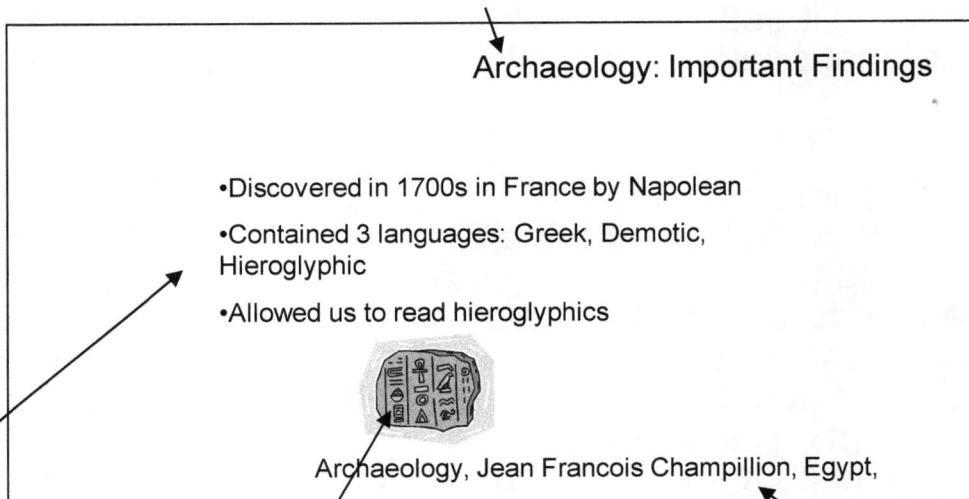

Archaeology: Important Findings

•Discovered in 1700s in France by Napolean

•Contained 3 languages: Greek, Demotic, Hieroglyphic

•Allowed us to read hieroglyphics

Archaeology, Jean Francois Champillion, Egypt,

Comprehensive definition. Not just what it is, but why its important

Other flashcards associated with this one

Picture you associated with term; can be stick figures; for example you might draw a crown if the flashcard was a king

Checklists: Weeks 1 and 2 Intro and Archaeology

Due Friday September 14

The Social Sciences
___ Lecture
___ Notes
___ Quiz

Skills of an Historian
___ Lecture
___ Notes
___ Quiz

Tools of an Historian
___ Lecture
___ Notes
___ Quiz

___ CR Reading   ___ Flashcards
___ Section Reviews ___ DT
   I commented _____ times.

Due Friday September 21

Archaeology Overview
___ Lecture
___ Notes
___ Quiz

Important Findings
___ Lecture
___ Notes
___ Quiz

No third lecture this week.

___ IL Worksheet   ___ Flashcards
___ Section Reviews   ___ DT
   I commented _____ times.

Parent Signature: _____

Mastery Test 1 Mastered on _____

Teacher Signature: _____

Checklist: Weeks 1 and 2 Early Man

Due Friday September 27

Very Early Man
___ Lecture
___ Notes
___ Quiz

Old Stone Age
___ Lecture
___ Notes
___ Quiz

Neanderthals
___ Lecture
___ Notes
___ Quiz

___ CR Reading   ___ Flashcards
___ Section Reviews ___ DT
    I commented ____ times.

Due Friday October 5

Cro-Magnon Man
___ Lecture
___ Notes
___ Quiz

Cave Paintings
___ Lecture
___ Notes
___ Quiz

Neolithic Revolution
___ Lecture
___ Notes
___ Quiz

___ CR Reading   ___ Flashcards
___ Section Reviews ___ DT
    I commented ____ times.

Parent Signature: _____

Mastery Test 2 Mastered on _____

Teacher Signature: _____

MLQ of the Day

Monday, _____/_____/_____
Q:

A:

_____

Tuesday_____/_____/_____
Q:

A:

_____

Wednesday _____/_____/_____
Q:

A:

MLQ 2

Thursday, _____/_____/_____

Q:

A:

_____

Friday, _____/_____/_____

Q:

A:

_____

Which news story from this week's CNN student news would you like more
   information on? Why?

Critical Reading

Citation:

Summary:

Critical Insight:

Critical Question:

The Social Sciences

History

- _____?
  - the story of the world's people once _____ was developed
  - before written history = _____

_____

- _____
  - how _____ influenced settlements and the course of history

Economics

- Systems of _____$$
  - how people make their _____
  - agricultural vs. industrial countries
    - Agricultural = _____
    - Industrial = _____
  - have vs. have-nots
  - _____
    - GNP = _____ _____

_____

- _____ and _____
  - how people's _____ affects the world
  - culture = _____

Political Science

- _____ and civics
  - how people _____
  - how to be a good citizen

_____

- Study of the _____ and development of man through the study of _____, _____, tools, etc.
- tries to explain _____

Skills of an Historian

Interpret fact vs. opinion

- Fact = statement that _____
  - Opinion

    _____
  - (cannot be proven)

Draw conclusions

- Using what you _____ plus what you _____ to guess what happened or what will happen next

See Cause and Effect

- Historical events do not happen _____
  - Actions always have

    _____

Recognize Points of View

- Two people may see the same event happen_____
  - Gender, social status, economics, geographical location and other things effect POV

Identify bias and prejudice

- Historical thinking can be clouded by our modern day judgments
  - Bias = _____, using pre-judgment to form opinion
  - Prejudice = any

    _____opinion or feeling, either favorable or unfavorable

Tools of an Historian

Primary Sources

- Are materials created _____ by people _____,
  - including photographs, paintings, documents, advertisements, music, films, and objects

Secondary Sources

- Are _____ by historians and others who use available _____ to _____.
  - They provide analysis and summary, placing events, people and evidence in historical context and asking questions about their meaning and significance

Time Lines

- Show how events occur _____
  - B.C/B.C.E → "0"
    - Years work towards "0"
    - B.C. = Before Christ
    - B.C.E = Before Common Era
  - A.D./C.E "0" →
    - Years work away from "0"
    - A.D. = Anno Domini
    - C.E. = Common Era

Maps

- Representation of Earth's features

Graphs

Charts

- Visual representations of data

Section Review

Flashcards: History, Geography, Economics, Sociology, Political Science, Anthropology, Fact, Opinion, Bias, Point of View, Primary Source, Secondary Source

1. Why is it important to study fields such as Political Science and Economics? How do these fields help us to understand history better?

2. Why is it important for an historian to be able to identify biases and prejudices? How do these things alter historical interpretations?

3. What is a primary source? How does it differ from a secondary source?

4. Explain how two people can witness the same event, but give a completely different interpretation of what happened? How does this come into play when we read an historians analysis of an event?

MLQ of the Day

Monday, ____/____/____
Q:

A:

_____

Tuesday____/____/____
Q:

A:

_____

Wednesday ____/____/____
Q:

A:

MLQ 2

Thursday, _____/_____/_____
Q:

A:

_____

Friday, _____/_____/_____
Q:

A:

_____

Which news story from this week's CNN student news would you like more
   information on? Why?

Archaeology Overview

Archaeology

- The study of the remains of past human _____
    - Began ~ _____ years ago
    - Europeans dug up Greek/Roman _____ and sold them

_____

- Things _____
    - Help us learn how people _____ long ago
    - Helps when no _____ can be found
- Do NOT have to be works of_____
    - Every day items
        - Tools, _____, pottery
    - Earliest artifacts = _____

Site

- Location where a "dig" is to take place
    - Archaeologists work closely with _____ to make sure it is OK to dig
    - _____ must be given

Excavate

- To dig into the earth; uncover remains of past

Date

- To find the age of remains
    - _____ first to divide human history into ages

Ages	• Used to divide early _____
	• Based on the material people used for tools and weapons
	○ _____
	▪ Divided into old, middle, new
	○ _____
	○ _____
Change in Division	• Archaeologists decided how people _____ = more important than materials for tools
	○ Early history divided into two periods
	▪ _____
	▪ _____
Tree Rings	• First way scientists dated archaeological finds
	○ Each year a tree grows a new ring
	▪ More rings = _____

Stop and Check for Understanding:

Flashcards: Arcaheology, fossil, artifacts, site, excavate, dating, ages

How do archaeologists divide early human history?

Important Findings

Italy in 1700s

- Discovery of two cities buried by the eruption of _____ in A.D. _____
    - Herculaneum
    - Pompeii
        - Evidence found of how early Romans actually lived.

_____

- Discovered in Rosetta, Egypt by Napoleon's troops
    - Inscribed w/ 3 languages
        - _____
        - _____ (everyday Egyptian)
        - _____ (religious Egyptian)
- Deciphered by Jean-Francois Champollion
    - it was the record of a _____ written in 196 B.C. praising King _____

_____

- Site in Tanzania
    - _____ more than 2 million years old
    - _____ found to be 3.7 million years old
    - Remains of 12 year old boy 1.65 million years old

What three languages were on the Rosetta Stone?

Olduvai Gorge

Color in the Map above and use an atlas or the internet to label as may of the following as you can (you should at least label Olduvai Gorge)

1) Taung, 2) West Turkana, 3) East Turkana, 4) Olduvai Gorge, 5) Peninj, 6) Hadar, 7) Laetoli, 8) Sterkfontein, 9) Swartkrans

Section Review

Flashcards: Pompeii, Vesuvius, Rosetta Stone, Olduvai Gorge

What is the difference between a fossil and an artifact?

What is the difference between an archaeologist and an anthropologist?

What two cities, later discovered in the 1700s, were buried by Mt. Vesuvius?
1.
2.

Name one example of "dating" that scientists and archeologists use to find out how old an artifact is:

What is the Rosetta Stone? What two major languages were on it? Why was it important?

MLQ of the Day

Monday, _____/_____/_____
Q:

A:

_____

Tuesday_____/_____/_____
Q:

A:

_____

Wednesday _____/_____/_____
Q:

A:

MLQ 2

Thursday, _____/_____/_____

Q:

A:

_____

Friday, _____/_____/_____

Q:

A:

_____

Which news story from this week's CNN student news would you like more
   information on? Why?

Critical Reading

Citation:

Summary:

Critical Insight:

Critical Question:

Very Early Man

65 Million Years Ago

- Humans _____ NOT live during the same time as dinosaurs
- _____ died out

3 Million Years Ago

- The first _____ like hominids appear
- The planet was teaming with life, 3 examples are:
    - _____
    - _____
    - _____

Very Early Humans

- Higher primates including _____ and early man first appear
- There were important differences between the two:
    - _____ could stand upright
        - _____ could not
    - Their _____ were different
        - Apes hands were made for _____ and _____
        - Human hands were jointed so that they could use _____

Lucy

- Discovered in _____ on the continent of _____
- 3 million years ago she would have been _____ tall and weighed _____
- She probably died from _____ in a lake

Fossils and Artifacts

- Fossils are _____ of _____ things (plants, animals, people), **not** man made
- Artifacts are remains of things that were _____ **not** living things

Old Stone Age

**Handy Man
(Homo Habilis)**

- One of the first hominids to use _____
- These people got their food from _____ and gathering
    - They did not plant crops, instead they gathered:
        - _____
        - _____

- _____ and _____ than Lucy's people
- Did _____ know how to make _____

**Upright Man
(Homo Erectus)**

- _____ know how to make fire, important because:
    - Now people could _____ their food
    - People gathered around the fire each night and shared _____ of the days hunt
        - = development of _____

- Same size as _____ humans
- Better tools including:
    - _____ and _____
- Did not have to worry about _____
- Made clothes from _____

Man Leaves Home

- About _____ years ago, man leaves Africa
- The _____ Age allowed them to _____ over giant frozen walkways

---

Flashcards: Lucy, Handy Man (Homo Habilis), Upright Man (Homo Erectus), Ice Age

Why was the ability to make fire so important?

Neanderthals

Neanderthals (Homo Sapien)

- Homo sapiens
  - Means "man who _____"
- Appeared about _____ years ago
- Named for the river in _____ where remains were first discovered
  - Have also been found throughout parts Asia and Africa
  - ~1 million thought to be living at the time

Good Hunters

- Used traps to catch birds and small animals
- Used _____ to catch large animals
  - Pitfall = large hole covered with branches
  - Once animal fell in they would kill it with a _____

Better Builders

- Made _____ by covering framework of mammoth bones with animal skins
  - Bones piled on the bottom prevented them from blowing away
  - As many as _____ people lived in a house during cold months
- Improved cave dwellings by digging drainage _____ and covering entrances w/ _____

Religion

- First people to _____ their dead

Flashcards: Neanderthal (Homo Sapien), Pitfall, Bury the Dead,

How did Neanderthals improve their living conditions?

MLQ of the Day

Monday, _____/_____/_____
Q:

A:

_____

Tuesday_____/_____/_____
Q:

A:

_____

Wednesday _____/_____/_____
Q:

A:

MLQ 2

Thursday, _____/_____/_____

Q:

A:

_____

Friday, _____/_____/_____

Q:

A:

_____

Which news story from this week's CNN student news would you like more information on? Why?

Cro-Magnon Man

Cro-Magnon Man
(EEMH)

- Named after a rock shelter in _____ where remains were discovered in _____
- Appeared in North Africa, Asia, and Europe
- Appeared ~_____ years ago
- Considered the first _____ human beings

Skilled Tool Makers

- Invented the _____
  o Ancient chisel
    ▪ Used to make other tools
- Used bone,_____, shells and wood for tools

_____

- Used antler bones to create sharper spears
  o Could fly faster and farther
  o Could stay greater distance from animals = safer
- **Better Hunters → increased food supply→ bigger population**

Invention of the Axe

- Used to cut down trees and hollow out logs for canoes
- In SE Asia used to cut bamboo for rafts
- Boats allowed them to travel on _____
  o Most likely how they reached Australia ~ _____ years ago

_____

- Carved statues out of ivory and clay
- Created jewelry out of shells
  o Decorated clothing with _____ beads
- Made _____and played music from hollowed out bones

Working as a Group

- Hunted in large _____
- Gathered yearly to exchange information about the movement of animals and to trade _____

See next lecture for Cave Paintings

Cave Paintings

Cave Paintings

- Many caves throughout Europe, Africa, and South America have been found
  - Covered w/ brightly colored paints made from minerals
- Pictures show mostly animals such as horses, bulls, and deer
- Many anthropologists think they have religions significance

Religion

- Believed that animals had spirits
- Painting a picture gave people power over the spirit
  - This would help them find and kill the animal
- Some cave paintings depict ceremonies, traditions, and history

Lascaux, France

- Discovered by _____ in _____
- Children playing in a field stumbled across the opening to a cave, inside the walls were covered with _____
-

Explore the Lascaux cave website. Choose 1 "panel" from the cave (for example the Hall of the Bulls). Write a story below about what you think is happening in the picture. Use lots of details and creativity. You may draw the picture to go with it if you wish.

Section Review

Flashcards: CroMagonon Man, Burin, Lascaux France, Cave painting, Invention of Axe

1. What is a hunter-gatherer?

2. What is a Stone Age?

3. Why was the ability to make fire so important?

4. How could early humans travel from Africa to Australia without a boat?

5. What did Cro-Magnon man paint on cave walls?

6.Why did Cro-Magnon man paint on cave walls?

Neolithic Age

Neolithic Revolution

- c. _____ B.C. People changed from food _____ to food _____
- 2 Important discoveries:
  - Grow Food
  - _____

_____

- Developed independently in different parts of the world
- People discovered that seed from wild grains could be planted and harvested

Herders

- First happened when hunting bands built _____ to enclose _____
- Farmers could kill _____ animal at a time and save the rest for later
- Captured animals began to lose their fear of people, this led to

_____

Food Producers

- Once people became producers they built _____ settlements

Early Villages

- Had _____ people in areas with good soil and _____

Neolithic Age cont.

Earliest Villages

- Jericho (present day Israel)
  - Dates to 8000 BCE
- Abu Hureyra (present day Syria)
  - Dates to 7500 BCE
- Catal Huyuk (present day Turkey)
  - Dates from 6500-5700 BCE

Catal Huyuk

- Struck by fire which blackened wooden and cloth objects
  - Helped _____ the objects

Early Houses

- Houses were made of _____ mud brick with flat roofs
- They used _____ to support the roof
- Each house had 2 or 3 rooms and no door
  - People went in and out through a hole in the_____

Specialization

- The development of _____
- Fewer people were needed to produce food so other jobs developed
  - Cloth weaving
  - Metal work

Neolithic Age cont.

Village
Government

- Land ownership develops and with it the protection of property

Chief

- Disputes were settled by a single chief who also along with a small group directed village activities
- Chiefs also served as village priests

Prayer

- At first Neolithic people prayed to forces of nature
- Later they developed gods and goddesses
  - Earth Mother was the most important, many houses had alters to her

Look up the word "revolution" in the dictionary or at dictionary.com. What does this word mean? Write a brief paragraph discussing whether or not the Neolithic Revolution was indeed a revolution. What other term could be used to describe this era?

Early Man Review

Flashcards: Neolithic Age, Neolithic Revolution, Paleolithic Age, Prehistory, Specialization, domesticated Civilization, Post-and-lintel, Earth Mother

1. What two important discoveries changed people from food gatherers to food producers?

2. What were two results of the increased food supply during the Neolithic age?

3. What two roles did village chiefs play?

4. How did learning to produce food lead to developing villages by early civilizations?

www.ingramcontent.com/pod-product-compliance
Lightning Source LLC
Chambersburg PA
CBHW062054090426
42740CB00016B/3129